# Love Pebbles

## Loving Reflections for the Soul

# Love Pebbles

*Loving Reflections for the Soul*

H. JAMES WILLIAMS

LOVE PEBBLES
Loving Reflections for the Soul

ISBN 13: 9780983434238
ISBN 10: 0983434239

LCCN: 2011904953

To purchase additional books:
www.aliantsecuritygroup.org
800.764.7114

Cover & Interior Design:
Anointed Press Graphics, Inc.
www.anointedpressgraphics.com
Copyright (c) 2011

# Dedication

Love Pebbles is dedicated to all who yearn to connect more deeply with others in a meaningful and spiritual way. More importantly it is dedicated to life and creation that together affords us each, whatever our lifetime, the opportunity to experience and know the benefits of love manifested in acts of kindness.

# Acknowledgment

I wish to acknowledge the Creator, and for me, the eminent source of all love.  To all who I have been blessed to know, personally and professionally, who have added to my personal reflections and perceptions of love.  To the love of family, teachers, writers and friends:  the cradle of support for anyone's personal appreciation and understanding of love.

# Introduction

Love needs no introduction. Human concept of the word is too expansive to be defined by any one individual. Each person ultimately comes to define the various aspects of love for his or herself in their own way. Love Pebbles was not written with the intent of attempting to concretely or absolutely define love for the human psyche. It was written merely to consider and reflect on a few of the "countless ways" that narrowly explore and reflect on aspects of love that bear truth to its intangible presence in our lives. May you find Love Pebbles to be inspirational and beneficial to this end.

*Let's Begin*

Intimate union of your body with
another is temporal. Intimate
oneness of your mind and spirit with
another is eternal. You only need
discern the difference to know
loving devotion.

Love is affectionate and gracious,
but it is also steadfast and just.

Loving Reflections for the Soul, 12

Love is selfless in its disposition and is embodied in goodness.

Deeds of love planted with wisdom reap harvests of loving-kindness.

Loving Reflections for the Soul, 14

Absent love the heart becomes like
stone and forfeits wholesome love of self
and love for others.

Loving Reflections for the Soul, 15

Love is even-tempered and a balm
to the soul.

Loving Reflections for the Soul, 16

Love is heaven's light in a world
of despair.

Loving Reflections for the Soul, 17

Love steadies the heart and mind
and conquers the fear of knowing
its tenderness.

Loving Reflections for the Soul, 18

Love is the bridge between souls over which faith and hope travel.

Loving Reflections for the Soul, 19

Love does not always reveal itself clearly, but it clearly reveals what it is not.

Loving Reflections for the Soul, 20

Love is the kinetic energy between souls.  It works respectively within us for the benefit of all.

Loving Reflections for the Soul, 21

Love is the kind portrayal toward others of your faith and belief in God.

Loving Reflections for the Soul, 22

Love is companionship with another in trust. Love is a partnership of your greater-self with the greater-self of another.

Loving Reflections for the Soul, 23

Every fulfillment of attraction, desire, passion and infatuation appeases the heart for a season.  Love's fulfillment continuously blossoms without season.

Love does not stray from the heart that in earnest honors it beyond condition.

Loving Reflections for the Soul, 25

Love is universal and beyond the concrete depth and comprehension of human understanding. Its explanations, similes and metaphors are many. Like rays of sunshine, love can only be radiantly given and received.

Love inspires inner-strength and greatness.  It lifts the soul to soaring heights.

Loving Reflections for the Soul, 27

Love is the road to eternal bliss
for those who lovingly, and with
patience of heart,
reverently travel its course.

Loving Reflections for the Soul, 28

That which fawns itself as love and is not faithful to a trust requiring little devotion, cannot be expected to love and remain faithful to a trust requiring unconditional devotion.

Loving Reflections for the Soul, 29

Love does not exploit or mislead for personal gain.  Love is transparent in design and finish.

Love not for money or gold. Love your choice of honorable labor to summon joy to your soul.

Loving Reflections for the Soul, 31

Love is a ladder with the height of its
ever increasing rungs allowing for a
more perfect view from the efforts
of its climb.

Deposit acts of love each day and love
will return you with dividends of love with
each tomorrow.

Loving Reflections for the Soul, 33

Love is the platform from which all human kindness and compassion are dispensed.

Loving Reflections for the Soul, 34

Love is at a minimum a single candle ablaze in the darkness. Love is at least a glimpse of light at the end of the tunnel.  Love springs from the eternal design of human purpose.  Love is the hope of goodness inspired by faith and manifested from the heart.

Loving Reflections for the Soul, 35

Love bears no one evil intent.
Love reproves for righteousness.

Loving Reflections for the Soul, 36

Love binds all families making up the
human family of life.
To supplant any one family, is to
supplant all mankind.

Loving Reflections for the Soul, 37

Mistakes and purposeful wrongs disappoint. Love redeems the repentant heart. Love resurrects and restores the brokenhearted to wholeness.

Loving Reflections for the Soul, 38

Love softens and smooths the
steppingstones lining the path across
its endless stream.

Love does not emanate from you.
Instead, you exist to channel love's
essence through you.

Loving Reflections for the Soul, 40

To discover and know the greater-love
residing within you, is to transcend
and know love's intimacy
beyond comparison.

Loving Reflections for the Soul, 41

Love is the birthright of every child.

Loving Reflections for the Soul, 42

Love wisely.
Love well.
Love with goodness of spirit.

Loving Reflections for the Soul, 43

Time now to continue along your
personally inspired path of love pebbles.
Simply begin with, "Love is . . ."

Remember to take time to give pause to,
and meditate on, your collections
along the way.

Loving Reflections for the Soul, 44

# About the Author

H. James Williams is a mentor, writer, speaker, entrepreneur, certified personal life coach and educator. He is the founder of Aliant Coaching Services and coaches individuals of all ages who are seeking personal and professional transformational changes in their lives.

He hopes Love Pebbles will enrich your life with deeper reflections of love to act with kindness toward your fellowman and to express love to the loved ones in your life.

For more information about Aliant Coaching Services or any H. James Williams products or services, go to www.aliantsecuritygroup.org.

Aliant Security Group
DBA:  Aliant Coaching Services
2702 Lighthouse Point East, Suite 621
Baltimore, Maryland  21224


www.aliantsecuritygroup.org
800.764.7114

www.ingramcontent.com/pod-product-compliance
Lightning Source LLC
Chambersburg PA
CBHW042059040426
42448CB00002B/68